NOTES

87992627R00061

Made in the USA
Lexington, KY
04 May 2018